My sun sets to rise again

Robert Browning; from 'The Mermaid'

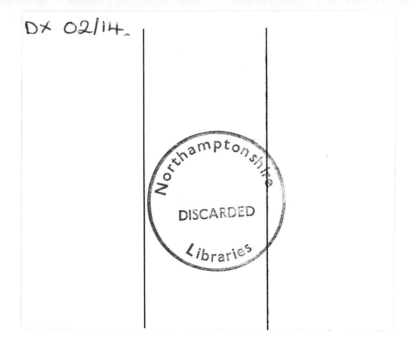
HONEY TREE

Published in Great Britain by Honey Tree 2013

Produced by Shore Books and Design

The moral rights of the authors have been asserted.

British Library Cataloguing in Publication Data. A catalogue record for this book is available from the British Library.

ISBN: 978 1 874392 29 3

Supported using public funding by
**ARTS COUNCIL
ENGLAND**

LOTTERY FUNDED

HEALING POETRY

Poetry Therapy

Foreword by Chris Tutton

This book is both a weapon and an antidote. It is an uplifting, honest, tender, touching and life-affirming collection which harnesses a resilient chorus of reassuring voices and provides hard evidence of poetry's ability to kindle resolve and to help beat depression into submission.

For some of the poets who feature on these pages and for more than three hundred and fifty million estimated global sufferers (WHO Oct 2012) depression, is a debilitating, insidious, pervasive condition which focuses on existing feelings of sadness and nourishes them with deeper uncertainties, self-recrimination and doubt. Life loses colour and spontaneity and the sufferer typically descends into an abyss of corrosive and destructive musings from which it becomes difficult to return. Habitual thought patterns become established which continuously release torrents of seemingly irrepressible negativity. Thoughts beget mood, mood begets condition and the struggle to identify an exit from the darkness becomes exhausting.

Usually the condition is met with limited understanding

and is typically treated, when it is treated at all, with a range of psychotropic medications which can indeed offer varying degrees of relief, but less real prospect of a cure. The furrow of habitually negative thought patterns often cuts deeper than the reach of such treatments alone.

The growing practice of administering poetry as therapy has persuasively suggested the potency of a more hollistic, natural and enduring treatment which uses the construction of image and verse as a vehicle for self expression and attaining enlightenment through perspective. Reading and writing poetry can afford the sufferer a vital measure of objectivity which may result in the identification and examination of the roots of suffering, thus offering the potential for constructive self analysis rather than self criticism.

American bibliotherapist, Perie Longo states that 'one of the benefits of poetry reading and writing is not only does it help us to define our essential 'self', but strengthen it. This is important if we are to feel a part of the world. And when we feel that we are not alone in the world, but are a part of it and integrated with it, esteem grows.'

Important new research by Dr Matthew Lieberman at the University of California has demonstrated that writing poetry helps the brain to regulate emotion unintentionally. The act of composing verse positively affects both the amygdala and the pre-frontal cortex, effectively reducing feelings of nervousness and sadness irrespective of the skill of the writer.

Not only has the practice of writing poetry proved effective in the treatment of depression, but as a means of therapy its application is simple, immediate, non toxic and within the reach of most people.

I am fortunate to have been awarded the opportunity to express and apply these principles in a recent nationwide series of Poetry as Healing workshops during which most of the poems in this book were written, not only by poets who may have been affected by depression, but by health care professionals, carers and others with a professional or personal interest in the subject.

As a result of my own observations of the development in the perspective of many people who attended these workshops over a number of months and the great deal of enormously positive feedback which I have subsequently received, I am greatly encouraged by the prospect of a wider acceptance of this method of helping to treat depression, and can unreservedly testify to the extraordinary healing power and potential of poetry as therapy.

C. T. August 2013

Contents

DUST OF SNOW

The way a crow
Shook down on me
The dust of snow
From a hemlock tree
Has given my heart
A change of mood
And saved some part
Of a day I had rued

Robert Frost

GO BACK

Go back to the song that's hidden in your heart,
Go back and find its melody and mode.
For have you not lost its flavour and breath
And life robbed the tune that would rise within you.
Go back, go back, it's never too late
To seek the place of music within.
So unique to you, its charm your being,
No songs the same, no melodies match.
Yet in harmony they come, sweetening the air
Lifting the gloom, lightening the heart.
For as we find that inner song,
An artist's orchestra will paint this world,
With beauty and love, with love and beauty.

Brian Allen

TO BEE...

I want to be a bee,
Sipping nectar from the flowers,
Hidden green pathways are my home,
My eyes see secret colours.
My sense of purpose is fixed and strong,
As I fly with the currents of the wind.
I know my place in the world.

Creating sweetness is my instinctive role,
Which I perform with skill,
No judgement, no right or wrong here,
Only fearless flight
Through a kaleidoscope world,
To the place where I belong.

Julie Darling

I AM TRYING TO FIND MY WAY

I am trying to find my way,
I wonder if I'll ever find my path,
I hear distant sounds, muffled and far away, like the
mother's voice through the walls of her uterus, softly
ringing 'come, come, come'!
I see that the only way to reach that place is to push hard,
make the monumental effort. To force energy through
these deadened limbs.
I want to break through MY life, my life, MY LIFE, my
life.
I am trying to find my way.
I pretend that I'm doing my wifely duties, but really I'm
planning my escape, 'The Great Escape', drizzling earth
from my trouser legs around the kitchen floor.
I feel I can bear it no longer.
I touch the membrane between this life and that, twang it,
feel it reveberate.
I worry I'll lose my resolve and never kick free, that as I
take flight I'll look back and see the rope tighten around
my ankle.
I cry, rarely (I find no tears). I cry "I'm going soon!"
I am trying to find my way.
I understand that I must be fully me, inflate like a
balloon. The helium of me-ness lifting me until I float
free, too big to fit back into this tiny life.
I say I know it sounds stupid, I sound stupid.

I dream of dark and loamy gardens, musty earthy smells,
honeysuckle air and rose petal beds (my garden, wild
and un-swept) and moist deep kisses, the poetry of life
trickling into my ears.
I try to improve my mothering, my health, to be as whole
as I can be.
I hope to make it through with the things I need intact.
I am trying to find my way.

Katrina Lay

THE STRAWBERRY

A man was being chased across a field towards a cliff by
a ferocious tiger. In order to escape he grabbed hold of a
vine and swung himself over the edge. When he looked
down, to his dismay, he saw two more tigers at the foot of
the cliff. Furthermore two mice were gnawing at the vine.
That's when he noticed a wild strawberry growing on the
cliff wall. He reached out, picked it and popped it in his
mouth.
It was the most delicious strawberry he had ever tasted.

Traditional Zen Story

WHY I WOULD LIKE TO BE A GIRAFFE

Giraffes are kind
and have enormous hearts.

Their long necks help
to keep their heads
Above the parts that
confuse and muddle.
Swivelling above the world
like periscopes,
their necks help them
to scan the space
below, behind and beyond.

Their coats have squares
that break things up
Into manageable sections.
Like sections of a quilt
that acts as camouflage
and hides them
from the common view.

Their tongues
are blue and friendly
but sure enough to wrap
around a sweet
high leaf and pull
it off the branch.

They are vegetarians.
They are non-violent.
They are sociable;
conspiring at times
like cranes on a building site.

They are nature's peace-builders.
They live at peace.
They are mindful,
elegant and gracious.
They will inherit the earth.

Louise Lotz

COLLECTIVE POEM

Clear horizons in the sunlight shine
The raindrops appear last thing at night
I am dazzled by the beauty of nature
Nature is cruel and yet beautiful!
Part of the world, part of us.

Coventry Workshop

COLLECTIVE POEM

Beneath I stand, beneath cool hoop of speckled
                                        green
Painted, washed with the sound of bird song breeze
The leaves will turn, then float away.
It's not that I want to hide, I just love to watch
Floating leaves on a windy journey
In pyramidic decay heaped in corners,
A sweet remembrance of two parallel scenarios of life
These leaves - these leaves are my life,
Seasons change, as do I
Remembrance is a lovely word.

Welwyn Garden City Workshop

THERE IS ANOTHER SKY

There is another sky,
Ever serene and fair,
And there is another sunshine,
Though it be darkness there;
Never mind faded forests, Austin,
Never mind silent fields -
Here is a little forest,
Whose leaf is ever green;
Here is a brighter garden,
Where not a frost has been;
In its unfading flowers
I hear the bright bee hum;
Prithee, my brother,
Into my garden come!

Emily Dickinson

WELCOME YOURSELF

A Woman
Hidden, covered, pushed under.
Disguised with layers of life
Where am I?
Who is she?
Where will she fit in?

Come on out,   step out
        Let me change your perspective
Be seen,   unlock
        Begin to unfreeze those layers
                of pain
                of hurt
                of circumstances
                of warped and twisted thoughts,

Step out,
Allow me to lead you
Into security in being yourself
Into F r e e d o m
Into expression
Into creativity
My love covers all you fear
Breaking down the barriers
some you have built.

Step out,   be seen
Welcome yourself
Be bold
Take courage
Be accepted.

Lyn Weaver

COLLECTIVE POEM

I wipe the mist from the window pane with my hand,
And I see clarity of vision.
A streak of light amidst the greyness.
What is it I am seeking? How am I to find it?

Trowbridge Workshop

COLLECTIVE POEM

He was sitting on the bridge holding an empty cup
"Thank you," he said as a coin was tossed in
Has that made you feel good?
Makes me feel completely useless - you can't eat or talk

                            to coins.
Food and drink make me strong.
It's the pull of the wind that I need to feel alive, and the
sound of the water rushing under the bridge,
The essence of the rain and sun combine to make you
                           grateful to be alive
So he looked again in the cup, it was frail porcelain and
through it he saw the world as if in a slow dance or a
fluttering leaf.

Leeds Workshop

A journey of a thousand miles begins with a single step

Lao Tzu

from Tao Te Ching, Chapter 64

WORN OUT

Like a wet cloth,
I have been wrung,
Until every drop
has been flung,
Leaving me drained and dry
of emotion and a cry.

I will fight on
To be courageous and strong,
To grind my teeth
for the sake of self-esteem.
The healing process will be long.
The God given strength I will accept.
To test and try.
To know not why.

But out of turmoil
Will come strength
To pave ways
To make amends
To give and take
To understand
The behaviour of destructive man.

Anne Untermoser

BEAR/SNAKE

Slithering along the ground, snarling
Baring teeth, hissing
Coiled round and round, tight
Buried deep, oblivious.
Explosive spring, unwound
Claws swiping, tongue flickering
Attacking the sunlit shadows
Defending the empty wound.

Susan Aiers

THE UNSPOKEN RULE

'You didn't tick the box to opt out' - said my keeper.
Initiation, induction - seduction.
Here is your uniform.
The only weapons we use, are the carrot and the stick.
We lead from the front, or we lead from behind.
The only bars in this prison, are in your mind.

Cynical Jo

THE RED WHEELCHAIR

Sitting in the corner of the room, graceless, alien
                                        and ugly
A threatening, complicated, hateful, untouchable thing
That must be touched, learned about, accepted.
A symbol to me of struggle, failure, anger.
I already hate it.
I HATE IT but have to be calm, composed, grateful.
Apparently it's the latest model, cost a lot of money.
Big fucking deal
But I smile, say thanks we'll give it a go
And watch as my son is introduced to his so-called
                                        independence.

Val Wright

SONG OF HOPE

O sweet To-morrow!
   After to-day
   There will away
This sense of sorrow
Then let us borrow
Hope for a gleaming
Soon will be streaming
   Dimmed by no gray -
   No gray!

While the winds wing us
   Sighs from the Gone.
   Nearer to dawn
Minute-beats bring us
When there will sing us
Larks of a glory
Waiting our story
   Further anon -
   Anon!

Doff the black token,
   Don the red shoon
   Right and retune
Viol-strings broken
Null the words spoken
In speeches of rueing
The night cloud is hueing
   To-morrow shines soon -
   Shines soon!

Thomas Hardy

COLLECTIVE POEM

The ball must bounce at your feet, the little ball of hope
How many times will it bounce?
It bounces high and it bounces low as he walks along the
                                    path
But the joy is that the ball
Bounces at all.

Welwyn Garden City Workshop

THE ORANG-UTAN

Poe casts me as a murdering beast.
But though my scruffy orange coat of finely tangled
fringes
And my earnest face are stricken from the beauty
pageant trail,
I care not that my strawberry blond tresses
Float the human presumption of ugliness personified.
I am redeemed by the compassion that nature provides.
I am an anthropomorphic phenomenon of intelligent
grace.
My attributes of human like behaviour allow me to
radiate
My loving empathic nature, as I nurture my perfect child.
I do not understand the cruel intolerance of humans.
My innocent eyes cry at their prejudice of aesthetic pride,
I feel rejected by the cold, cruel world of their
sterile beauty,
This prostitute of the human soul also destroys my
dwelling place,
Plundering, murdering with bestial disgrace.

Susan Morrell

COLLECTIVE POEM

The carnival masks of Venice were aquired during the
                    same misty February visit.
It was cold, but the masks did not show what was really
                                        there
I can be me but no one knows it's me dancing and free
How afraid I am
As I stand before them, but I am me
I expect people to take me as I am
But society does not work like that.
The people can judge me as much as they like,
But now I don't really care as my response is on strike.

Taunton Workshop

THE WONDERER
(ONE WHO WONDERS)

I am a small piece of the furniture of the universe,
I wonder if my spirit lives forever,
I hear time passing in the voices of my children
I see the future burning at the edges of the present
I want the valley, the lake, the song of birds,
I am the wonderer proclaiming I am,
I pretend I have been to the mountain,
I feel the love between the moon and the deep blue sea,
I touch your body to feel I am alive,
I worry that I won't return,
I cry there will only be a hell to return to,
I am a mourner, a rider on a pale horse,
I understand the catastrophe diamond and how nothing is
    really understood,
I say beauty is found in the absence of the human,
I dream of the golden sunshine days and the smell of
    meadows,
I try to be patient,
I hope I may be wrong,
I am just a part of it all.

Andrew Henry Smith

I SEE A UTOPIA

I am a definition of myself, I wonder why that is,
I hear the wind calling my name but then it goes away,
I see a utopia of being but it's not really there,
I want to ask why you can't have this,
I am a definition of myself.
I pretend to listen, but don't understand
Does it make me look bad?
I feel great at breakfast time,
I touch the very thing that's life and it feels,
I worry if its not there and cry for all mankind,
I am a definition of myself,
I understand when things go bad,
Don't try to fix when it's not broken,
I say but does it really change,
I dream of a better time in the space
Time continuum,
I try to hold everything in one hand
When you have two,
I hope I don't drop what I've been given,
I am a definition of myself.

Paul Henry

LEISURE

What is this life if, full of care,
We have no time to stand and stare.
No time to stand beneath the boughs
And stare as long as sheep or cows.
No time to see, when woods we pass,
Where squirrels hide their nuts in grass.
No time to see in broad daylight,
Streams full of stars, like skies at night.
No time to turn at Beauty's glance,
And watch her feet, how they can dance.
No time to wait till her mouth can
Enrich that smile her eyes began.
A poor life this if, full of care,
We have no time to stand and stare.

W H Davies

SEPTEMBER

September is a pregnant month
Sifting hope from dying embers
Laying to rest old enigmas,
Where dreams had risen to limited vistas
Splashing strange colours on the passing plethora,
But holding not that which is timed.
So much must fall before new sights rise
Taking away once clutched at ways,
And drawing a line for season change
Where the unseen can claim its ground.
We have not always wanted this passing,
For pain is too close to a dying.
But nature has hidden ways, gentle urgings,
Promptings of hidden callings
Unveiled and discovered
By the passing pilgrim.

Brian Allen

FOX

Slinking back to the house in early dusk
beneath the moon and slate-grey rooftops
I pad along the beaten path,
hear the wind high in the treetops.

Vixen and cubs greet my return
her narrow eyes and bared-teeth I scan,
She nuzzles her face; I'm pleased to know,
I'm still her silver-haired-fox-of-a-man...

Mark Randles

WHO AM I?

I am an amoeba so I could be anything.
I can change, adapt and be quite acceptible.
It just came into my head and with only 6 mins 27
seconds to consider this question................
So the good news is that there are lots of us
We can live almost anywhere and have been around for a
long time and, like the dandelions, are likely to flourish
whatever happens externally.
Now all this freedom, is it good? Why not? What does it
matter?   That's it.

Elizabeth

COLLECTIVE POEM

I heard a young man sing today
How it stilled, then danced, lilting within me.
His song was one of freedom,
it released me from my own captivity,
The music cascading wildly through my brain.
I sit now and listen, forgetting lists,
There's nothing needs my time.
His voice, my listening, blending as one,
Dropping my spirit, covering cares, releasing the real me,
And singing a song within us all.

Bristol Workshop

PEACE

Peace and happiness is the way to be
Rather live in the moment than be unhappy
So I live the best I possibly can
And be positive every day
And I lived in a memorable place
Where I was in peace and harmony
Practicing my morals and living care free
Because that's how I thought life should be.

Ravinder Raj

THE NEST

The nest was flat and splindly like a chimney
                                       sweep's brush.
Now exposed to the world and its dangers.
The men had come to her tree and noisily butchered its
                                       branches.
'It's only a pigeon', they said.
'It's a rubbish nest', they said.
As soon as they left, she flew back to her eggs.
She sat and guarded them
Through rivers of rain and buffeting winds.
Through noisy nights.
She sat and watched and waited.

I watched and waited with her.
And her mothering made me remember
And feel things I didn't want to feel.
I'd thought I would be like her.
But my tiny, newly hatched beauties
Didn't have the warmth of a wing to snuggle under
Didn't have the calm and watchful eye
or the unquestioning, unswerving love.
They had me.
Twisted, angry, fighting
Blind and unseeing.

If I could do it again
I would do it like her.
My nest may not look the best
But it would be warm and safe.
I would weather the stinging rain and the numbing cold.
I would nourish and teach
Kindly
And let my young be young.
When it was time for them to fly
I would watch them go
Knowing they were ready and prepared.
And I would feel a pride and a sadness and an
                                    acceptance
Sitting up high, in the middle of my empty nest.

Nicky Rumble

LEOPARD

I saw a leopard once
In the wild.
It was difficult to see,
Lying on a branch
Out in plain view but
Hidden behind its spots.
Languorous and unconcerned,
Watching me
Knowing at any time it could melt
With no thought
Into the density
And not be caught up,
Taken and shaken,
By the darkness, the chaos
Of the jungled mess.
It can slip through, slip in quiet,
Crossing the screeching, pulsing, pullulating,
                              quick-darting,
Going nowhere, life,
And still be its own being
Grounded and free
And utterly at one with itself.

Susan Aiers

THE WHITE HIND

White shape against the hill,
Like an ancient symbol carved in chalk.
She stands, frozen,
A moment of stillness,
As she sniffs the air and tests the wind.
She's broken cover,
Emerged from the wild wood,
Where green shadows
Protect and shield her.

A cloud moves across the hill,
An insubstantial shadow,
That creeps across the moor.
She's startled,
She jumps,
Barks a defensive warning.
She moves,
Fleet of foot,
Agile, delicate and strong,
She jumps the high wall
And is gone.

Julie Darling

HONEYSUCKLE

I will weave the hedge this May,
I will warp and weft my way,
Back and forth my shuttle green -
Weaving, spinning country cream.

I will loop and lark the hedge,
As cool trout leap the water's edge.
I will arc and spool along -
Soft colour of mediaeval song.

My loom the winter long did wait
To thread the bobbin and create
All summer long
My honeysuckle cradle song.

Damask rose and white I made,
And now my yarn in sun and shade
Will clothe the hedge and strew the air
With scented garlands - sweet and fair.

tory

DESERT PULL

The desert scares me with its bleakened space
So different from my rested pose,
It frightens me with non-agenda
And scares me with its spacious grasp.
I step right in, but just one step
Then look for ways to make that void.
This pulling and pushing, this back and forth,
They tangle my life, and leave me raw
I try again, its two steps now,
A pattern forms of in and out,
And which will win I cannot say,
But this I know from day to day,
It draws, it pulls, it draws me in.

Brian Allen

WHERE TO GO FOR FEAR

I am full of fear.
I wonder if I will ever be free of it.
I hear my heart beating too loudly in my chest.
I see only a path of confusion and darkness.
I want to feel the sun in my heart.
I am full of fear, full of fear.
I pretend to smile and smile until my face breaks in two.
I feel my feet slipping.
I touch the ground that bears me.
I worry that it cannot carry me.
I cry out, "Then let me sink".
I am nothing more than the earth that bears me.
I understand nothing, I stand under nothing.
I say, "Be still, be still, BE STILL!"
I dream of emptiness.
I try but I would rather be.
I hope we can be friends, this fear and me.
I am coming to be.

Susan Aiers

STOPPING BY WOODS ON A SNOWY EVENING

Whose woods these are I think I know,
His house is in the village, though;
He will not see me stopping here
To watch his woods fill up with snow.

My little horse must think it queer
To stop without a farmhouse near
Between the woods and frozen lake
The darkest evening of the year.

He gives his harness bells a shake
To ask if there is some mistake.
The only other sound's the sweep
Of easy wind and downy flake.

The woods are lovely, dark and deep,
But I have promises to keep,
And miles to go before I sleep,
And miles to go before I sleep.

Robert Frost

BAT

Being a bat I'd like to be
Hanging around so nobody can see
What thoughts go round inside of me.
Because being a bat I can fly free
Using my senses as I fly around
Through the air without a sound
Not even having to touch the ground
As I gather up the insects that I have found
No-one can touch me, because I won't let them near
I fly through the air without any fear
I'm amongst friends that are to me dear
I don't have to think who's on my rear
I have one thing on my mind
That is to eat and live
But if anyone bumps into me
I will then forgive
Because not everyone has eyes in the back of their arse
For to me this life has been made and caste
For I am black as black as night
For in myself I have this fight
This fight to survive
Which is my right
I will come through the dark
To be seeing the light!

Linda Colegrave

COLLECTIVE POEM

Deep red rose caressed by morning dew
Dripped a splattered message onto the stone floor,
Marker of the dawn of a new day with hope
"Water" it said, "Water is life"
After a year of grief and unending pain, new hope had
finally emerged within me,
Just a little guidance, such a lot of hope.
The rose withered down in the ground only to rise again
The dew, new, returns to the petals.
A rose once mistaken for a bramble was cut off to the
                                    ground,
Feared dead and gone;
The following year up it sprang far bigger and better than
                                    before.

Welwyn Garden City Workshop

PING PONG BALL

Battered from pillar to post - at the mercy of my host.
Hit on the side of the head, battered about,
            battered about - do I count for owt?
Where will I land next? - I don't know which way to go.

Battered about, battered about - from pillar to post, at the
            mercy of my host.

Hit against objects, not knowing where I will land.
Cause and effect? - I do not know.
No control - in the hands of the dealer.

I'm an inaminate object, that's what I am,
I have no control, I am unable to shout 'stop'.
I am delicate, like a precious bird's egg - but could easily
            be crushed by a strong man's hand.

As I am so delicate, why am I being treated with such
            force and brutality?
Why does my dealer yell in rapturewhen he deals me
            a blow?
Why does he leap in the air and 'put a spin on it'?
Is he getting gratification from this?
I am hit against walls and hard surfaces.
No dents or cracks to show.
Give me a break - before I break.

Cynical Jo

LYING

How can all this fit inside one skin?
The feelings.
Some I recognise (we're on first name terms)
Some are darker; shapeless and moving.
Just out of reach.
Slowly, creeping,
Or pouncing, then taking hold.
They wrap and suffocate and squeeze.
All I can do is stand and breathe and wait.
Or bang and crash and rage.
Is it just me?
Maybe I've been given the wrong skin?
Too thin, too weak, too frightened.
I watch.
Watch others with their daily ease and their doing
                              everything inside their skin.
A smooth, sunny crossing.
I watch from the eye of the storm. Holding on.
I join them for a while.
But the sky is darkening and lowering and murmuring.
Then it starts again
And I'm not like them.
I'm a howling, writhing she-monster.
With thin skin
And too many feelings that won't lie down
And behave.

Nicky Rumble

SIGNIFICANT ME

"your contemplations will never be more than
dreams..." (*)

Significant me! What a fable!
Of all the grains of sand...
I'm caught in the 20s frenetic hangover.

I'm busy, busy, busy;
part of the have less's, new, have more's,
exercising my new found affluence.

My wants are insatiable,
but what more could I need;
I'm clothed, fed and housed...!

I dream and dream, but can't afford to dream.
Life passes me by, and at 76,
not much more of it is left.

''Time wasted is not wasted!''
But is it not wasted?
So many ideas left unexplored;

But why are they important?
It's my life; it's how I am...
It's how I am!

Projects take on a life of their own
until exhausted,
then replaced, *ad infinitum*...

High metabolistic me;
high then low adrenalin;
high energy, then very low energy.

But am learning how to pace myself...

Barry Fox

(*) From 'A Day of Judgement' by Chris Tutton,
'Angles of Repose' 2012

COLLECTIVE POEM

When I was young I dreamt all day
And some of my dreams came true but not all
Some of them are still ripening in the cinnamon depths,
Some of them have fallen to the wayside or taken from
me and others materialized.

Trowbridge Workshop

A HOPE CAROL

A night was near, a day was near,
  Between a day and night
I heard sweet voices calling clear,
  Calling me
I heard a whirr of wing on wing
  But could not see the sight;
I long to see my birds that sing,
  I long to see.

Below the stars, beyond the moon,
  Between the night and day
I heard the rising falling tune
  Calling me:
I long to see the pipes and strings
  Whereon such minstrels play:
I long to see each face that sings,
  I long to see.

To-day or may be not to-day,
  To-night or not to-night,
All voices that command or pray
  Calling me,
Shall kindle in my soul such fire
  And in my eyes such light
That I shall see that heart's desire
  I long to see.

Christina Rossetti

COLLECTIVE POEM

There is no starting point other than the start.
It can be that most of us cannot even see the start
Lost in the labyrinth of uncertainty and fear,
Tied down by words and thoughts we should not hear
But inside your head a voice sings -
a solitary bird on the brink of dawn
A tree that stands and takes your breath
Sturdy Oak, how I envy your strong roots.

Leeds Workshop

MY TOKEN ANIMAL

Sleep the snowy sleep of winter
Frost nips your eyelash glint
Ice it creeps and creeps its signature
Honest comfort in the whiteout bleak
Time over time, snow, you come and go.

Jana Vera Greasley

I AM...

I am the mad woman who dances in the Dene,
                    eats leaves and sings,
I wonder where I come from and where I'll be tomorrow.
I hear the call of home as I browse sweet saplings in the
                    wood,
I see green and gold with whispering shadows
                    underneath.
I want to be free, to know joy and the lightness of being.
I am the mad woman who dances in the Dene,
                    eats leaves and sings.

I pretend all is well, that the wounds are all healed,
                    with no cracks showing,
I feel unknowing, wise and insubstantial,
I touch the edge of light and the hem of shadow.
I worry when ravens draw close, with sharp beaks and
                    harsh voices;
I cry at beauty, tears of sorrow held deep in the dark pool
                    of grief.
I am the mad woman who dances in the dawn,
                    eats leaves and sings.

I understand the pull of the tide, but not that of people,
I say the safe words, too scared to speak truth.
I dream of that place where I know I belong, light and
                    leafy, with the sound of the sea,

I try to tread carefully, learn the steps of life's dance,
I hope dawn will come, blessing me with the light of
life's lessons.
I am the wise woman who dances in the dawn, eats
leaves and sings.

Julie Darling

COLLECTIVE POEM

In the heat of the day and the cool of the evening
I sit alone - and watch and wait
Hoping for dreams to come true?
Or planning to make them come true?
Or for the honeysuckle scent to fill the air and draw in
the searching bee.

Trowbridge Workshop

HARE

A bounding hare
Boxing in the fields
With all its fierce full-moon madness
On display
Proudly
A creature of magic
Of fertility of the mind
And the body - sinews twisting -
So much energy
Bounding, leaping
Joyful
Alive.

Wendy Attwell

THE TIGER

I would like to be a tiger
Such symmetry as described by William Blake
Tyger, tyger, burning bright,
In the forest of the night
Respected and feared, such a dangerous deadly beauty,
Combining strength and speed
Pacing the forests and jungles with such arrogance and
                                        self confidence
Needing to be fearful of few beasts.
Except maybe man!

Neil Newcombe

The man who removes a mountain begins by carrying
away small stones.

Chinese Proverb

MESSIER 31: KO1701.04
POETRY AT THE END

I would appear as
an alien animal
a descending angel
in which something of me remains
a dark soul perhaps

The world is confounded
by my alien form
Steeples fall
towers topple
hair torn from the roots
and the zaqqum tree embraced

Cracks become fissures in the brainwash
radicalising everybody's final moments
language telepathene transformative

My consort;
at my side
a supermassive black hole
surely a God!

Andrew Henry Smith

UNTITLED

Passing the day lumbering,
A good mother to your child
Now at least, since the text books have caught up
65 million years out of date and counting.
Eating quietly above all the
Proto-birds squarking and jabbering around you.
Remembered, fondly, but sleeping now.
You lucky thing.

Paul Regan

COLLECTIVE POEM

To be true to me whilst not alienating others
Is a struggle harder than I can imagine
But I fought and think I found a way through
Though the path I forge closes behind me, unique.
Leaving the pain, finding the light, locking that out
And so much depends on small details like the sunlight
                              on the floor
Reaching toward me as I yearn towards it.

Welwyn Garden City Workshop

COLLECTIVE POEM

"Repeat after me", said the man,
"I believe I am always right."
But sometimes a voice of doubt creeps in,
Oh, how I could stop, change direction.
I turn this way, then I turn that,
Forgetting what was first said.
"Repeat after me", said the man,
"It's really alright to be wrong!"
But there's more: a place beyond to be either right or
wrong
Just being satisfied, content, free to be me.
"Repeat after me", said the man.

Bristol Workshop

No man is an island,
Entire of itself.

> *John Donne*
> *from 'For Whom The Bell Tolls'*

THE OLD CIRCUS LEOPARD

It's an old wound troubles me each October.
These grey, English skies; the damp;
Haloween and the clocks going back -
These days I live with a limp.

When I ran
through woods that night
Wild wind harassing
bright clouds of leaves
the world mad with rage
shaking branches
of neon lit trees -
who was that horseman
riding away?
I never saw him again.

Next day I returned to where you lay,
brother cub who never changed his spots.
There was no flicker of recognition
before your long and final exhalation.

Terry Simpson

THE SUBALTERNS

"Poor wanderer," said the leaden sky,
"I fain would lighten thee,
But there are laws in force on high
Which say it must not be."

--"I would not freeze thee, shorn one," cried
The North, "knew I but how
To warm my breath, to slack my stride,
But I am ruled as thou."

--"To-morrow I attack thee, wight,"
Said Sickness. "Yet I swear
I bear thy little ark no spite,
But I am bid enter there."

--"Come hither, Son," I heard Death say;
"I did not will a grave
Should end thy pilgrimage to-day,
But, I, too, am a slave!"

We smiled upon each other then,
And life to me had less
Of that fell look it wore ere when
They owned their passiveness.

Thomas Hardy

TIGER

Tiger, No, No never
Powerful Explosive
Isolated Feared avoided
But wait   Change comes
Isolation thaws
Fears melted by love
Avoided no longer
Power turned - channelled
Tempered with grace
Moving in a new direction

Lyn Weaver

HOPE IS THE THING WITH FEATHERS

Hope is the thing with feathers
That perches in the soul,
And sings the tune--without the words,
And never stops at all,

And sweetest in the gale is heard;
And sore must be the storm
That could abash the little bird
That kept so many warm.

I've heard it in the chillest land,
And on the strangest sea;
Yet, never, in extremity,
It asked a crumb of me.

Emily Dickinson

In the midst of winter, I found there,
was, within me, an invincible summer.

Albert Camus
from 'The Stranger'

Acknowledgements

'Dust of Snow' and 'Stopping by Woods on a Snowy Evening' taken from the Poetry of Robert Frost, edited by Edward Connery Latham, published by Jonathan Cape. Reprinted by permission of the Random House Group.